An Open Heart for Love

Rosa Purcell

WestBow Press books may be ordered through booksellers or by contacting:

WestBow Press
A Division of Thomas Nelson & Zondervan
1663 Liberty Drive
Bloomington, IN 47403
www.westbowpress.com
844-714-3454

Scripture quotations marked NIV are taken from The Holy Bible, New International Version®, NIV® Copyright © 1973, 1978, 1984, 2011 by Biblica, Inc.® Used by permission. All rights reserved worldwide.

ISBN: 978-1-6642-6579-0 (sc)
ISBN: 978-1-6642-6772-5 (hc)
ISBN: 978-1-6642-6580-6 (e)

Library of Congress Control Number: 2022908325

Print information available on the last page.

WestBow Press rev. date: 08/27/2022

WestBow
PRESS®
A DIVISION OF THOMAS NELSON
& ZONDERVAN

Love is a heart.

Being able to love is the best part of you.
It gives life meaning.

Love opens your eyes,
makes you notice the stars,
and changes you.

It makes you wish for good things to happen
to someone besides yourself.

And there are many different ways to express it . . .

It's a teacher who pushes you to do your best
and encourages you to have big dreams,
ones that you never thought were possible.

Love is a friend who knows all your flaws,
but only remembers what makes you unique.

It's a brother who loses at playing a board game,
so his sister knows what it feels like to win.

It's giving a Christmas gift to someone you will never know,
just to make that person smile.

It's saying a kind word to brighten someone else's day,
even when you are sad yourself.

Love is a newborn baby your dad takes care of, even when he is so tired he can barely stay awake.

It's a warm bowl of soup your mom makes on a cold day
when you're feeling sick.

It's eating freshly baked cookies with Grandma
and watching a baseball game with Grandpa.

Sometimes love looks like a rainbow at the end of a bad day,
or a bright, sunny day after a rainstorm.

Sometimes it's a butterfly that flutters around your head
as you try to catch it.

Love refreshes your soul, like the sound of ocean waves on a summer day, or the smell of blooming flowers.

It's a puppy who waits all day for you to come home
so that you can give each other hugs and kisses.

Love is saying you're sorry when you hurt someone's feelings, and meaning it.

Even more importantly, it's forgiving someone who hurt you and giving that person a second chance.

It's accepting people as they are
and giving them room to grow.

It's praying for someone who is suffering.

It's helping the helpless.

Love is making a promise to someone and, even when it's hard, keeping that promise.

Love is the Earth that God made for us
to share with each other,
and all of its beautiful creatures.

It's a precious gift from God.

And the most important thing about love
is choosing to open your heart
so you can share it with everyone.

And now these three remain:
faith, hope and love.
But the greatest of these is love.
1 Corinthians 13:13 (NIV)

Printed in the United States
by Baker & Taylor Publisher Services